Beyond the Players
Mascots

by Allan Morey

Bullfrog Books

Ideas for Parents and Teachers

Bullfrog Books let children practice reading informational text at the earliest reading levels. Repetition, familiar words, and photo labels support early readers.

Before Reading
- Discuss the cover photo. What does it tell them?
- Look at the picture glossary together. Read and discuss the words.

Read the Book
- "Walk" through the book and look at the photos. Let the child ask questions. Point out the photo labels.
- Read the book to the child, or have him or her read independently.

After Reading
- Prompt the child to think more. Ask: Mascots are people in costumes. They are part of the team. If you could be a mascot, what sport would you be a mascot for? What would your name be?

Bullfrog Books are published by Jump!
5357 Penn Avenue South
Minneapolis, MN 55419
www.jumplibrary.com

Copyright © 2024 Jump! International copyright reserved in all countries. No part of this book may be reproduced in any form without written permission from the publisher.

Library of Congress Cataloging-in-Publication Data

Names: Morey, Allan, author.
Title: Mascots / Allan Morey.
Description: Minneapolis, MN: Jump!, Inc., [2024]
Series: Beyond the players | Includes index.
Audience: Ages 5–8 years
Identifiers: LCCN 2023022272 (print)
LCCN 2023022273 (ebook)
ISBN 9798889966470 (hardcover)
ISBN 9798889966487 (paperback)
ISBN 9798889966494 (ebook)
Subjects: LCSH: Sports team mascots—Juvenile literature.
Classification: LCC GV714.5 .M67 2024 (print)
LCC GV714.5 (ebook)
DDC 796—dc23/eng/20230518
LC record available at https://lccn.loc.gov/2023022272
LC ebook record available at https://lccn.loc.gov/2023022273

Editor: Jenna Gleisner
Designer: Emma Almgren-Bersie

Photo Credits: lev radin/Shutterstock, cover, 20–21, 23bl; Tracy Evans/Dreamstime, 1; kcube - kaan baytur/Shutterstock, 3; Andy Martin Jr/Alamy, 4; Randy Litzinger/Icon Sportswire/Getty, 5; Dustin Bradford/Getty, 6–7, 13, 23br; Cal Sport Media/Alamy, 8–9; Robert Blakley/Dreamstime, 10–11, 23tl; PA Images/Alamy, 12; Hunter Martin/Getty, 14–15, 23tr; jane/iStock, 16; Joshua Rainey/Dreamstime, 17; Richard T Gagnon/Getty, 18–19; Jerry Coli/Dreamstime, 22tl; Aspenphoto/Dreamstime, 22tr; James Kirkikis/Dreamstime, 22bl; Richard Paul Kane/Shutterstock, 22br; Ron Hoff/Dreamstime, 24.

Printed in the United States of America at Corporate Graphics in North Mankato, Minnesota.

Table of Contents

Go Team!	4
Part of the Team	22
Picture Glossary	23
Index	24
To Learn More	24

Go Team!

We are at a hockey game.

Look! The mascot skates. He leads the cheer!

Mascots are part of the team.

A mascot is a symbol.

It stands for the team.

This team picked a lion. Why?

Lions are strong!

Mascots are fun.
They cheer.
They get fans excited!

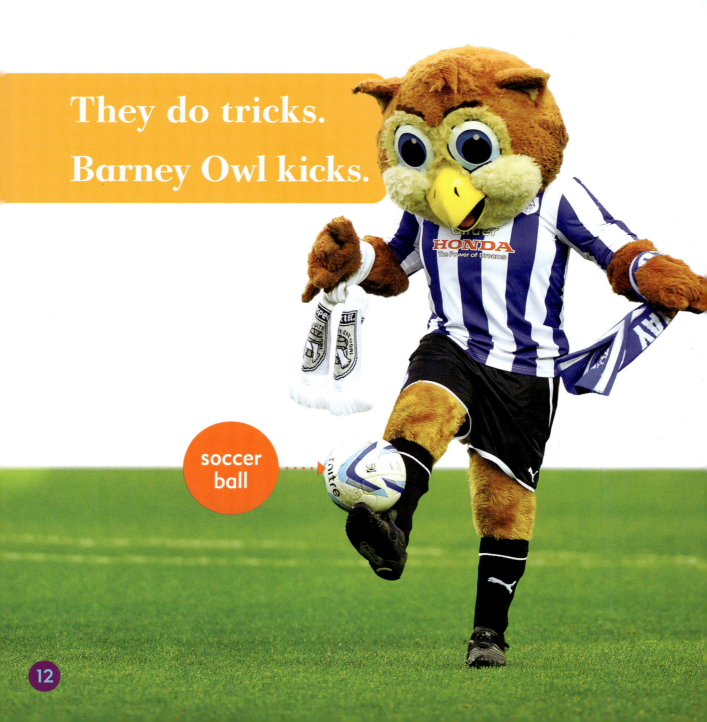

They do tricks.
Barney Owl kicks.

soccer ball

Dinger drives.

They are funny.
Phillie Phanatic jokes.
He makes fans laugh.

This team is losing.

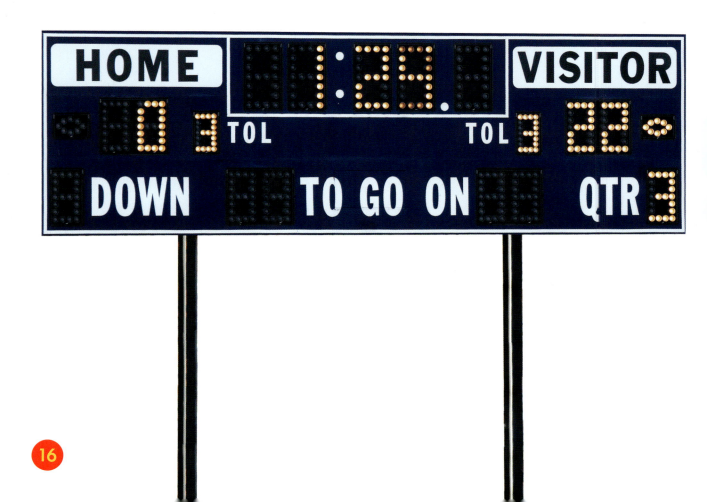

**The Duck shouts.
Go team! Get a touchdown!**

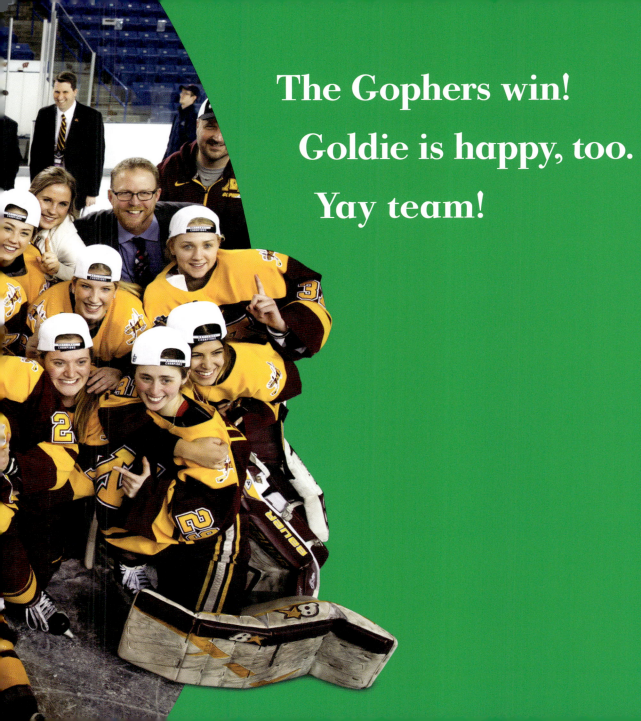

The Gophers win!
Goldie is happy, too.
Yay team!

Can you be a mascot?

Yes!

You just need team spirit!

Part of the Team

Mascots are part of the team. What do they do? Take a look!

celebrate
Mascots cheer with fans when their team scores or wins!

cheer
Mascots clap, dance, and move!

play
Mascots play with fans. They are friendly and fun!

perform
Mascots show off. They get fans excited!

Picture Glossary

cheer
To praise or encourage with shouts.

fans
People who are very interested in or enthusiastic about something.

spirit
Courage, enthusiasm, and determination.

symbol
An object or design that stands for, suggests, or represents something else.

Index

cheer 5, 10
fans 10, 14
fun 10
funny 14
game 4
leads 5
shouts 17
spirit 20
symbol 6
team 6, 9, 16, 17, 19, 20
tricks 12

To Learn More

Finding more information is as easy as 1, 2, 3.

❶ Go to www.factsurfer.com

❷ Enter "mascots" into the search box.

❸ Choose your book to see a list of websites.